Francis Frith's
SCOTTISH CASTLES

PHOTOGRAPHIC MEMORIES

Francis Frith's
SCOTTISH CASTLES

◆

Clive Hardy

FRITH
BOOK Co

First published in the United Kingdom in 1999 by
Frith Book Company Ltd

Text and Design copyright © Frith Book Company Ltd
Photographs copyright © The Francis Frith Collection

The Frith photographs and the Frith logo are reproduced under licence from Heritage
Photographic Resources Ltd, the owners of the Frith archive and trademarks

British Library Cataloguing in Publication Data

Scottish Castles
Clive Hardy
ISBN 1-85937-077-2

Frith Book Company Ltd
Frith's Barn, Teffont,
Salisbury, Wiltshire SP3 5QP
Tel: +44 (0) 1722 716 376
Email: sales@frithbook.co.uk

Printed and bound in Great Britain

CONTENTS

FRANCIS FRITH: *Victorian Pioneer*

FRANCIS FRITH, Victorian founder of the world-famous photographic archive, was a complex and multitudinous man. A devout Quaker and a highly successful Victorian businessman, he was both philosophic by nature and pioneering in outlook.

By 1855 Francis Frith had already established a wholesale grocery business in Liverpool, and sold it for the astonishing sum of £200,000, which is the equivalent today of over £15,000,000. Now a multi-millionaire, he was able to indulge his passion for travel. As a child he had pored over travel books written by early explorers, and his fancy and imagination had been stirred by family holidays to the sublime mountain regions of Wales and Scotland. 'What a land of spirit-stirring and enriching scenes and places!' he had written. He was to return to these scenes of grandeur in later years to 'recapture the thousands of vivid and tender memories', but with a different purpose. Now in his thirties, and captivated by the new science of photography, Frith set out on a series of pioneering journeys to the Nile regions that occupied him from 1856 until 1860.

INTRIGUE AND ADVENTURE

He took with him on his travels a specially-designed wicker carriage that acted as both dark-room and sleeping chamber. These far-flung journeys were packed with intrigue and adventure. In his life story, written when he was sixty-three, Frith tells of being held captive by bandits, and of fighting 'an awful midnight battle to the very point of surrender with a deadly pack of hungry, wild dogs'. Sporting flowing Arab costume, Frith arrived at Akaba by camel seventy years before Lawrence, where he encountered 'desert princes and rival sheikhs, blazing with jewel-hilted swords'.

During these extraordinary adventures he was assiduously exploring the desert regions bordering the Nile and patiently recording the antiquities and peoples with his camera. He was the first photographer to venture beyond the sixth cataract. Africa was still the mysterious 'Dark Continent', and Stanley and Livingstone's historic meeting was a decade into the future. The conditions for picture taking confound belief. He laboured for hours in his wicker dark-room in the sweltering heat of the desert, while the volatile chemicals fizzed dangerously in their trays. Often he was forced to work in remote tombs and caves where conditions were cooler. Back in London he exhibited his photographs and was 'rapturously cheered' by members of the Royal Society. His reputation as a photographer was made overnight. An eminent modern historian has likened their impact on the population of the time to that on our own generation of the first photographs taken on the surface of the moon.

VENTURE OF A LIFE-TIME

Characteristically, Frith quickly spotted the opportunity to create a new business as a specialist publisher of photographs. He lived in an era of immense and sometimes violent change. For the poor in the early part of Victoria's reign work was a drudge and the hours long, and people had precious little free time to enjoy themselves.

Most had no transport other than a cart or gig at their disposal, and had not travelled far beyond the boundaries of their own town or village. However, by the 1870s, the railways had threaded their way across the country, and Bank Holidays and half-day Saturdays had been made obligatory by Act of Parliament. All of a sudden the ordinary working man and his family were able to enjoy days out and see a little more of the world.

With characteristic business acumen, Francis Frith foresaw that these new tourists would enjoy having souvenirs to commemorate their days out. In 1860 he married Mary Ann Rosling and set out with the intention of photographing every city, town and village in Britain. For the next thirty years he travelled the country by train and by pony and trap, producing fine photographs of seaside resorts and beauty spots that were keenly bought by millions of Victorians. These prints were painstakingly pasted into family albums and pored over during the dark nights of winter, rekindling precious memories of summer excursions.

THE RISE OF FRITH & CO

Frith's studio was soon supplying retail shops all over the country. To meet the demand he gathered about him a small team of photographers, and published the work of independent artist-photographers of the calibre of Roger Fenton and Francis Bedford. In order to gain some understanding of the scale of Frith's business one only has to look at the catalogue issued by Frith & Co in 1886: it runs to some 670

pages, listing not only many thousands of views of the British Isles but also many photographs of most European countries, and China, Japan, the USA and Canada – note the sample page shown above from the hand-written *Frith & Co* ledgers detailing pictures taken. By 1890 Frith had created the greatest specialist photographic publishing company in the world, with over 2,000 outlets – more than the combined number that Boots and WH Smith have today! The picture on the right shows the *Frith & Co* display board at Ingleton in the Yorkshire Dales. Beautifully constructed with mahogany frame and gilt inserts, it could display up to a dozen local scenes.

POSTCARD BONANZA

The ever-popular holiday postcard we know today took many years to develop. In 1870 the Post Office issued the first plain cards, with a pre-printed stamp on one face. In 1894 they allowed other publishers' cards to be sent through the mail with an attached adhesive halfpenny stamp. Demand grew rapidly, and in 1895 a new size of postcard was permitted called the

court card, but there was little room for illustration. In 1899, a year after Frith's death, a new card measuring 5.5 x 3.5 inches became the standard format, but it was not until 1902 that the divided back came into being, with address and message on one face and a full-size illustration on the other. *Frith & Co* were in the vanguard of postcard development, and Frith's sons Eustace and Cyril continued their father's monumental task, expanding the number of views offered to the public and recording more and more places in Britain, as the coasts and countryside were opened up to mass travel.

Francis Frith died in 1898 at his villa in Cannes, his great project still growing. The archive he created continued in business for another seventy years. By 1970 it contained over a third of a million pictures of 7,000 cities, towns and villages. The massive photographic record Frith has left to us stands as a living monument to a special and very remarkable man.

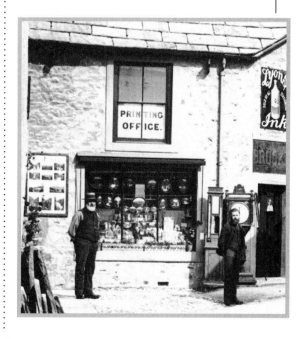

Frith's Archive: *A Unique Legacy*

FRANCIS FRITH'S legacy to us today is of immense significance and value, for the magnificent archive of evocative photographs he created provides a unique record of change in 7,000 cities, towns and villages throughout Britain over a century and more. Frith and his fellow studio photographers revisited locations many times down the years to update their views, compiling for us an enthralling and colourful pageant of British life and character.

We tend to think of Frith's sepia views of Britain as nostalgic, for most of us use them to conjure up memories of places in our own lives with which we have family associations. It often makes us forget that to Francis Frith they were records of daily life as it was actually being lived in the cities, towns and villages of his day. The Victorian age was one of great and often bewildering change for ordinary people, and though the pictures evoke an impression of slower times, life was as busy and hectic as it is today.

We are fortunate that Frith was a photographer of the people, dedicated to recording the minutiae of everyday life. For it is this sheer wealth of visual data, the painstaking chronicle of changes in dress, transport, street layouts, buildings, housing, engineering and landscape that captivates us so much today. His remarkable images offer us a powerful link with the past and with the lives of our ancestors.

TODAY'S TECHNOLOGY

Computers have now made it possible for Frith's many thousands of images to be accessed almost instantly. In the Frith archive today, each photograph is carefully 'digitised' then stored on a CD Rom. Frith archivists can locate a single photograph amongst thousands within seconds. Views can be catalogued and sorted under a variety of categories of place and content to the immediate benefit of researchers. Inexpensive reference prints can be created for them at the touch of a mouse button, and a wide range of books and other printed materials assembled and published for a wider, more general readership - in the next twelve months over a hundred Frith local history titles will be published! The

See Frith at www. francisfrith.co.uk

day-to-day workings of the archive are very different from how they were in Francis Frith's time: imagine the herculean task of sorting through eleven tons of glass negatives as Frith had to do to locate a particular sequence of pictures! Yet the archive still prides itself on maintaining the same high standards of excellence laid down by Francis Frith, including the painstaking cataloguing and indexing of every view.

It is curious to reflect on how the internet now allows researchers in America and elsewhere greater instant access to the archive than Frith himself ever enjoyed. Many thousands of individual views can be called up on screen within seconds on one of the Frith internet sites, enabling people living continents away to revisit the streets of their ancestral home town, or view places in Britain where they have enjoyed holidays. Many overseas researchers welcome the chance to view special theme selections, such as transport, sports, costume and ancient monuments.

We are certain that Francis Frith would have heartily approved of these modern developments, for he himself was always working at the very limits of Victorian photographic technology.

THE VALUE OF THE ARCHIVE TODAY

Because of the benefits brought by the computer, Frith's images are increasingly studied by social historians, by researchers into genealogy and ancestory, by architects, town planners, and by teachers and schoolchildren involved in local history projects. In addition, the archive offers every one of

us a unique opportunity to examine the places where we and our families have lived and worked down the years. Immensely successful in Frith's own era, the archive is now, a century and more on, entering a new phase of popularity.

THE PAST IN TUNE WITH THE FUTURE

Historians consider the Francis Frith Collection to be of prime national importance. It is the only archive of its kind remaining in private ownership and has been valued at a million pounds. However, this figure is now rapidly increasing as digital technology enables more and more people around the world to enjoy its benefits.

Francis Frith's archive is now housed in an historic timber barn in the beautiful village of Teffont in Wiltshire. Its founder would not recognize the archive office as it is today. In place of the many thousands of dusty boxes containing glass plate negatives and an all-pervading odour of photographic chemicals, there are now ranks of computer screens. He would be amazed to watch his images travelling round the world at unimaginable speeds through network and internet lines.

The archive's future is both bright and exciting. Francis Frith, with his unshakeable belief in making photographs available to the greatest number of people, would undoubtedly approve of what is being done today with his lifetime's work. His photographs, depicting our shared past, are now bringing pleasure and enlightenment to millions around the world a century and more after his death.

SCOTTISH CASTLES – *An Introduction*

THE NORMANISATION OF SCOTLAND

CASTLE BUILDING came to mainland Scotland not as a result of conquest and occupation, but as a result of the deliberate policies of kings like Malcolm III and David I, who encouraged the immigration of Anglo-Norman lords by offering land grants. Both Malcolm and David were influenced by what they had seen during their stays in England. Following his father's death, Malcolm had spent a number of years as an exile at the great Anglo-Norman court of Edward the Confessor. The Norman influence on David was even stronger; having been brought up and educated at the English court, he was keen to import Norman society and the Norman-style government and feudal tenure into Scotland. When he returned north, among the many friends who came with him were Bernard de Balleul, Robert de Brus and Walter FitzAlan.

Under David the Anglo-Norman lords built motte and baileys with timber towers as they had in England, and within fifty years Norman lords were holding lands as far north as the Don, Spey and Moray. Native landowners still held their lands, but now they were tenants, bound by feudal obligations to render services to their overlords. However, what is interesting is that these lords did not rebuild their fortresses with great stone keeps as they did south of the border; in fact, the most northern castle with a classic Norman keep is at Norham on the Tweed.

William the Lion, who reigned from 1165 to 1214, built castles at Ayr, Lanark and Dumfries in order to keep the Lords of Galloway in check, and he built Dunskaith on Cromarty Firth and Redcastle on Beauly Firth during his attempt to extend his rule. In the areas of Scotland under Norse rule there were a handful of castles in existence during the 12th century, but castle building did not assume any importance until the reign of Haakon IV. The 'Orkneyinga Saga' recalls the building of a small stone castle on the island of Wyre in the Orkneys by Kolbein Hruga around 1143-48; this was the place where the murderers of Earl John Haraldson fled to in 1231. Today this castle is better known as Cubbie Row, a corruption of Kolbein's name. The small tower has walls 5 ft thick and is protected by ramparts; there was no entrance to the ground floor from the outside. Other Norse castles in the Orkneys are Damsay (in existence in 1136) and Cairston (besieged 1152). Dunvaig Castle on Islay might also be of Norse origin.

By the beginning of the 7th century the site occupied by Edinburgh Castle was a stronghold of the Gododdin, but in 638 it fell to the Northumbrians, at the time the most powerful of the Anglian kingdoms whose territory now stretched from the Forth to the Humber and to the south of the Mersey. Edinburgh would later become the principal residence of Malcolm III and his wife Queen Margaret, though the earliest surviving structure, Queen Margaret's Chapel, comes from the reign of David I. Few of the royal castles retain much of their original features, though when besieged by Edward I in 1296, Edinburgh may have been one of the most advanced castles of the day, along with Bothwell and Kildrummy. The natural features of the site were incorporated into the plan so as to make the best possible use of them.

THREE ROYAL CASTLES

◆ ◆

Even today Edinburgh Castle looks impregnable. However, an inherent weakness in the defences was the lack of water. The fortress is perched high on a cliff of carboniferous basalt, and the main well is 89 feet deep. Though supplies under normal conditions were adequate, excessive demand during periods of dry weather would lead to it drying up. Following the castle's capture in 1314, Bruce ordered it to be slighted so as to render it of no further military use to the English. The well was filled in and its location lost. It was not rediscovered until 1381.

Edinburgh has been the focus of a number of sieges, and has been in English hands more than once. In 1296 Longshanks deployed giant catapults to batter the garrison into submission; they surrendered after three days and nights of rock-dodging. In 1314 it was recaptured for the Scots by Thomas Randolph, Earl of Moray, from Peres Lebaud, Edward II's Sheriff of Edinburgh. An assault force led by William Francis made their way along an old track up the north precipice, scaled the walls, opened the gates, and let the main force in. Twenty-one years later, the castle, or what was left of it, was occupied by Edward III's troops under Guy, Count of Namur. Guy managed to hold on to the ruins for just a day and a night before being forced to surrender, but within a few months the English were back - and they intended to stay.

They successfully held out against Sir Andrew Moray in 1336, only to fall in April 1341 to a cunning plan devised by William of Douglas. He and his men disguised themselves as merchants bringing supplies to the garrison. They dropped their loads so that the gates could not be closed; then they held on until joined by the main force, whereupon they took the castle. Of the English garrison of 49 men-at-arms, 60 archers and six watchmen, most were butchered, their bodies flung over the walls onto the crags where they were left to rot.

Sir William Kirkcaldy of Grange had been appointed by the Regent, Lord James Stewart,

English. For Mary, her reign would be an unhappy one: she was a Catholic monarch in a state gradually undermined by Calvinism. Her marriage to the Dauphin ended with his death; her second marriage to Darnley was a disaster that ended with his assassination; her relationship and marriage to the womanizing Earl of Bothwell fuelled open rebellion, and

Earl of Moray, to hold Edinburgh Castle in the name of James VI. Whilst riding through Linlithgow on 23rd January 1570, Moray was shot by James Hamilton. The assassin fired his piece from the window of a house belonging to the Archbishop of St Andrews, who incidentally appears to have supplied the getaway horse. The Archbishop was later executed at Stirling: money was saved by his not being granted the formality of a trial. Even before Moray's death Sir William was shifting his allegiance to Mary, Queen of Scots, and by mid-1571 was openly supporting her.

It had been from Dumbarton Castle that five-year-old Mary, Queen of Scots had left for France, where she was to wed the Dauphin in return for French aid to rid Scotland of the

there were demands that she be burnt. Her abdication in July 1567 in favour of her young son James VI plunged the country into a brief, and for Mary disastrous, civil war. In May 1568 she crossed into England, heir-presumptive to Elizabeth I, and, had she resisted the temptation to plot with Catholic nobles, she might well have succeeded in regaining her throne. Though Mary remained in England for the rest of her life, Dumbarton Castle was held in her name until it fell to Sir Thomas Crawford of Jordanhill in 1571. Only Edinburgh Castle was to hold out longer.

When the ruthless but extremely capable James Douglas, Earl of Morton was appointed Regent, he laid siege to Edinburgh. The castle was well defended, it had the best artillery in Scotland, and money and military aid had been sent by Charles IX of France. In January 1573 Morton received help from Elizabeth of England. She placed her best fortifications and military engineers at Morton's disposal. They surveyed the fortress and reported that 'we find that there is no mining that can prevail in this rock but only battery with ordnance to beat down the walls and so make to climb'. The report was taken on board: six batteries of English artillery under the command of Sir William Drury, Governor of Berwick-upon-Tweed, were sited at various locations around the castle. The bombardment was opened on 16 May 1573, and the castle was pounded. David's Tower partially collapsed blocking the garrison's vital water supply, the Constable's Tower was shot to pieces and an infantry assault was made on the Spur. The garrison finally surrendered on 29th May, and the redoubtable Sir William and his brother were executed.

In the aftermath of the siege of 1573 a vast amount of money was lavished on Edinburgh Castle, both to upgrade its defence capability and to improve the royal apartments. The great Half-Moon Battery was built, wrapped round the remains of David's Tower; the Forewall Battery was remodelled; and the Portcullis Gate was constructed. The Portcullis Gate was completed in 1577; it is also known as Morton's Gate, as it was constructed during the regency of the Earl of Morton. It replaced the 14th-century Constable's Tower, badly damaged during the siege. The decorative upper part of this building is not as old as it looks, for it was added in 1886-87. The royal palace which dated from the early 15th century was reconstructed in 1617. However, the greatest period of construction dates from the 18th century. The Queen Anne Building, together with Drury's and Butt's batteries, were all added around 1708-13; the perimeter wall above the crags was built in stages between 1730-37; the Governor's House and the Cart Sheds date from the 1740s; and the Ordnance Stores and the North Barracks from the 1750s. The New Barracks were added during the Napoleonic Wars.

It is not known with any certainty if Stirling was a stronghold of the Gododdin, though a history of Scotland published in 1527 states that Kenneth MacAlpin besieged a castle there in 842. Stirling was a royal castle during the reign of Alexander I and he is thought to have died there in 1124. Along with Edinburgh, Roxburgh, Berwick and Jedburgh, Stirling was ceded to Henry II following the capture and imprisonment of William the Lion. There is, however, no firm evidence that Stirling was garrisoned with English troops at this time. In 1296, on his march north, Edward Longshanks found Stirling abandoned save for a gate-keeper. It was held by the English, but retaken the following year by William Wallace and Andrew Murray after the garrison had been starved into surrendering. Stirling was again abandoned by the Scots following Wallace's defeat at Falkirk. Once again the English took possession, strengthening the fortifications. It fell to the Scots again in 1299, and by 1303 it was the only major fortress in their hands. In 1304 the garrison, commanded by that able campaigner Sir William Oliphant, were besieged by Longshanks himself. The English king settled down for a long siege. He ordered a floating bridge built so the Forth could be crossed at a lower point, and he deployed no less than seventeen siege engines. Oliphant surrendered on 20th July; Longshanks was not amused. He had spent a great amount of money on a new siege engine known as 'the war wolf', and he wanted value for it. Part of the garrison was ordered to remain in the castle while the 'wolf' was tried out. Longshanks must have been satisfied with the result, as the 'wolf' virtually demolished the gatehouse. We are not told what state the garrison was in after being on the receiving end of the bombardment.

In the 16th century Stirling would play a major part in the unhappy events surrounding Mary, Queen of Scots and her son James VI. In 1571 there were rival parliaments in Scotland: supporters of the young King met at his residence, Stirling, while his mother's loyal followers met at Edinburgh. On the night of 3 September 1571, Sir William Kirkcaldy of Grange attacked Stirling in the hope of capturing those who had attended the parliament there.

Stirling Castle also underwent a number of structural changes. When the forework was remodelled for James IV, it partially followed the line of earlier defences. The main gatehouse was an imposing structure with a three-quarter round tower at each of its four angles and a semi-circular tower on either side where it joined the curtain wall. The high curtain wall was in its turn supported by a rectangular tower at either end. The Prince's Tower, which still stands almost to its original height, was built slightly away from the precipice. The Elphinstone Tower, of which just two floors survive, may have been where the castle's senior officers lived, as it was fitted with at least one kitchen. Alas, this tower was dismantled during the late 17th century. The gatehouse has also been greatly reduced. The two inner towers were demolished, as were the

16

semi-circular ones, while the two outer towers now stand at less than half their original height.

James V also spent a lot of money on Stirling Castle. Apart from refurbishing old buildings and apartments, James also ordered the construction of a new palace block under the administrative eye of Sir James Hamilton. The palace abuts the Prince's Tower; it contains apartments for both the king and queen, as well as an attic storey which probably provided accommodation for certain officers of state. It is set out on three sides of a rectangular courtyard sometimes known as the lion's den. This might refer to the lion finials on the gable ends, or to the fact that a lion was bought for the king in 1537 and might have been housed here at some time or another.

The first documented evidence for a castle at Balmoral dates from 1484, when it was known as Bouchmorale and held by Alexander Gordon, second son of the first Earl of Huntly. By the end of the 18th century it was owned by the Earl of Fife, and in 1830 it was leased by Sir Robert Gordon. Sir Robert hired the architect William Smith to remodel the old castle, and extensions were built to provide additional accommodation and new kitchens. Smith also added a turreted tower. Queen Victoria and Prince Albert made their first visit to Balmoral in September 1842. Victoria fell in love with the place because she loved the walks and rides the estate offered; Albert because it reminded him so much of his native Thuringia. Following Sir Robert's death in October 1847, Victoria and Albert were offered Balmoral - but there was a problem. The royal couple were not personally wealthy, and though £31,500 was found to buy the estate, they had precious little money left

to carry out alterations. Help came from a most unusual source. The eccentric barrister John Camden Neild bequeathed Victoria £500,000 'for her sole use and benefit', and it is thanks to Neild's generosity that Balmoral exists in the form it does today. Prince Albert hired William Smith, and together they worked on creating one of the finest examples of Scottish baronial architecture. Built of Invergelder granite quarried on the Balmoral estate, the castle comprises two ranges joined by an 80 ft tower and is able to accommodate up to 120 people.

TOWER-HOUSES

Tower-houses exist throughout Scotland and Ireland. The earliest appear to have been constructed in the later 13th to mid 14th centuries. Usually standing four or five storeys high, they are in effect a rethink of the medieval hall-house: instead of being a series of rooms extended horizontally, here they are stacked vertically for defence. Internal arrangements varied - it often depended on how much the owner was prepared to spend - but towers did represent good value for money in that they were strong enough to withstand most forms of attack apart from sieges.

The walls of the tower were usually thickest at ground floor level, both to support the weight of the structure and for defence. The ground floor was usually vaulted for protection against fire, and in some towers the only access to this level was by an internal staircase or ladder. The main entrance was a door on the first floor reached by a ladder which could be taken inside when danger threatened. Usually this floor contained the hall and the private chamber of the owner. As fire was often used by raiders, those owners who could afford it had their towers roofed with slate or stone. Over a couple of centuries the tower-house developed from a simple rectangular type, such as those at Loch Leven and Threave, to an L-plan, where either one or two flanking wings were added; these not only provided extra accommodation and storage space, but made possible flanking fire along up to three sides of the main block. There then followed the Z-plan towers. Here two projecting jambs were built, echeloned diagonally opposite to one another. The result was that the castle was now fully flanked at little extra cost. The jambs were either two round towers, two square ones, or one of each, and they were not necessarily of the same height. Z1 examples with two round towers include Terpersie, Powrie and Claypotts. Z2 examples with one square and one round tower include Ballone and Moncur; Z3-plan castles with two square towers, of which there are twenty-three known examples, include Hatton, Glenbucket and Noltland. There were a number of variants which combined elements of both L and Z types built from the late 16th century, one of which was an L-plan house with a projecting semi-circular stair turret on the rear wall.

BORDER RAIDERS AND REIVERS

For centuries the exact border between Scotland and England was difficult to define. Even William the Conqueror's Domesday commissioners did not go north of the Tees; and during the reign of his son William Rufus, England's northern border might well have followed the line of Hadrian's Wall, its

focal points being the fortresses of Carlisle to the west and the New Castle on the Tyne over to the east.

During the reign of David I, Scotland's border with England was on the Tees; the land had been won not through force of arms but by skilful diplomacy. Later, when Henry II insisted that Northumbria be returned to England, William the Lion launched an invasion, but he was unfortunately captured at Alnwick and carted off to the fortress of Falaise in Normandy. William acknowledged Henry as his feudal lord, and a number of castles in southern Scotland were ceded to the English. By the end of the reign of Edward I, the border was on a line from Carlisle to Berwick, both sides divided into three marches, each of which was governed by a Warden. The idea was that the Wardens would maintain law and order and meet with their respective opposite numbers in order to resolve any problems affecting their areas of control. That was the idea, but the practice was often different. There was also a vast expanse of land inland from the Solway Firth that was claimed by both crowns, though neither had any effective control over it.

Years and years of devastation resulting from the coming and going of Scottish and English armies had reduced the Borders to a lawless no-man's-land where raiding, cattle reiving and sheep lifting had become a way of life. The Borderers themselves were not organised by nationality; Scots raided Scots, English raided English, Scots joined forces with English Borderers to raid other Scots and so on. Also, there were a number of Border clans such as the Maxwells, Johnstones, Douglases, Armstrongs and Crichtons who not only wreaked havoc throughout the area, but fought pitched battles against one another or were drawn into blood feuds that could last for decades.

Many of the Wardens were no better, often mounting raids of their own. However, there were truce days when both sides met at an appointed place and matters were resolved without men reaching for their swords. One truce that degenerated into a pitched battle was at Reidswire in the summer of 1575. The English were represented by their middle march warden Sir John Forster, a cunning old rascal in his seventies; his opposite number on the Scottish side was Sir John Carmichael, keeper of Liddesdale. After several hours of fairly amicable conversation an argument developed, which led to the exchange of insults and then of blows. With one man dead, the wardens managed to calm down their followers; but suddenly the Scots jumped the English, capturing old Sir John and killing his deputy Sir George Heron. The English Borderers opened fire with longbows, cutting down a number of Scots; the Scots in turn were reinforced by the arrival of men from Jedburgh, many no doubt carrying murderous Jedburgh axes with 4 ft long blades. It was the Scots' turn to attack, and they routed the English.

The castles in the Borders are for the most part tower houses on the Scottish side and Northumbrian peles on the English. Powerful clans such as the Maxwells were able to build fortresses such as Caerlaverock, seven miles south-south-east of Dumfries, while the Douglases were responsible for fortifying Hermitage Castle. Throughout the Borders farmers, who were not only on the receiving end of raids even from their own countrymen, but were often raiders and reivers themselves, took to building bastels for their protection. These were stone-built farmhouses, usually two-storey; their name is derived from the French word bastille, a small fortress. The basement was for cattle and stores, the upper floor for domestic quarters. Those who could afford it built their bastels with barrel-vaulted basements and stone or slate roofs, as raiders often resorted to the use of fire. Even if raiders gained access to the basement, the vaulting was tough enough to prevent them from breaking into the domestic quarters and butchering its occupants. The windows of the basement were the smallest possible, allowing in the bare minimum of light and ventilation. Those in the domestic quarters were protected with iron bars.

Hermitage Castle stands alone amid the barren hills of Liddesdale in the middle march of the Borders. The earliest reference to it dates from 1296, when it was held by the Comyns. Ownership eventually passed to the Dacres, who demolished the old fortifications and built what was in effect a Northern English fortified manor house comprising a tower and central court enclosed by a cross-wing and walls. Later remodelling saw the demolition of the Dacre tower and its replacement by a larger one, together with corner towers and an oblong wing. The castle was also equipped with bell-mouthed gunports. Liddesdale was a wild enough place for Hermitage to have its own keeper; in 1566 the post was held by James, Earl of Bothwell, and lover of Mary, Queen of Scots. Bothwell was once badly wounded tackling a reiver; Mary rode the forty miles from Jedburgh in a single day to be at his bedside. She subsequently caught a fever and nearly died.

With the accession of James VI the pacification of the Borders began. Troops poured into the area, and justice was often swift and brutal. The reivers were effectively put out of business by 1610.

GLOSSARY OF TERMS

Bailey: defended courtyard or ward of a castle.

Barbican: gated outer work, usually separated by a drawbridge from the main gate of the castle.

Bastion: a work at an artillery fortification that allows defenders to fire along the flanks of the fortification.

Crenellation: licence to crenellate and raise a fortified building.

Curtain: wall enclosing a bailey, ward or courtyard.

Keep: the great tower of a castle, also known as a donjon.

Machicolation: openings in the floor of a projecting parapet that allowed the defenders to drop missiles upon the heads of attackers.

Motte: mound on which castle was built; usually artificial.

Murder holes: openings in ceilings through which attackers could be shot at.

Portcullis: heavy grille made of wood and/or iron protecting an entrance. It was raised or lowered by winches in the gatehouse.

Ringwork: circular or oval shaped defensive bank and ditch surrounding a hall.

EDINBURGH CASTLE 1883 E24303

BOTHWELL CASTLE 1897 39867

Bothwell is acknowledged as one of the finest examples of secular architecture in Scotland, though it was never completed to its original design. Bothwell's design is similar to the stronghold of Coucy in that it has a round donjon, as do Kildrummy and Dirleton. Dirleton was built about 1225 by John de Vaux, seneschal to Marie de Coucy.

BOTHWELL CASTLE 1897 39866

The surviving inner half of the round donjon can be seen in the background. It stood 82 ft high, was 65 ft in diameter, and the walls were 15 ft thick. Bothwell was taken and retaken a number of times; in 1298-99 it was under siege for fourteen months before the Scots managed to take it, only to lose it again in 1301. It remained in English hands until the time of Bannockburn, when it surrendered to Edward Bruce.

BOTHWELL CASTLE 1897 39865
Overlooking the Clyde to the north of the present town of Bothwell, the castle is still an impressive sight despite being a ruin. Following its slighting in 1337, Bothwell lay waste until 1362 when it was refortified. Excavations here have uncovered the largest assemblage of medieval pottery so far found on a single site. Some of it is of local manufacture, some of it English.

BRAEMAR CASTLE c1960 B266001
This is a five-storey L-plan tower-house built by the Earl of
Mar in 1628. It was here in August 1714 that a so-called hunt
was assembled by John Erskine, sixth Earl of Mar. It was in
fact the start of a rebellion against the house of Hanover and
the Union, and the Stuart standard was raised. Though
Braemar had been burnt by Graham of Claverhouse in 1689,
it had been rebuilt. The curtain wall was added when the
castle was used as a garrison for government troops.

BRODICK BAY AND CASTLE, ARRAN 1890 A93002

CAWDOR CASTLE, 1890 C212001

BRODICK BAY AND CASTLE
Arran 1890
Now owned by the National Trust for Scotland, Brodick Castle, once the seat of the Dukes of Hamilton, dates from the 14th century. It was from here in 1307 that the Bruce launched his campaign to liberate mainland Scotland from the English. Brodick was enlarged when garrisoned by Cromwell's troops, and the tower is a mid 19th-century addition.

◆

CAWDOR CASTLE
1890
The central tower of the castle dates from a licence of 1454 when the thane was permitted to erect Cawdor 'with walls and ditches and equip the summit with turrets and means of defence, with warlike provisions and strengths ....Provided that it would always be open and ready for the King's use and his successors'. Cawdor is traditionally the scene of Duncan's murder by Macbeth, Thane of Cawdor.

CROOKSTON CASTLE
Paisley 1897 39808

Crookston was the first property to be acquired by the
National Trust for Scotland. The estate was held in the
12th century by Sir Robert Croc of Neilston, and it is
from him that the castle derives its name. In the 14th
century the estate passed into the hands of Alan Stewart
of Darnley; the tower was probably built in the early
15th century by Sir John Stewart, Constable of the Scots
in the French service. In July 1565 Henry, Lord Darnley
and Mary, Queen of Scots came to Crookston following
their marriage. The castle at that time was owned by
Darnley's father the Earl of Lennox.

DOUNE CASTLE FROM THE BRIDGE 1899 44645
Situated to the south-east of the town on the left bank of the river Teith at its junction with the Ardoch, Doune Castle derives its name from the Gaelic word 'dun', meaning a fortified place. It differs from the earlier great castles such as Kildrummy and Bothwell in that the living apartments are incorporated into the gatehouse. In older castles the practice was to position them to the rear of the courtyard.

DOUNE CASTLE, FROM THE NORTH-EAST 1899 44646
Doune was conceived as a courtyard castle, but was never finished. It was built by Robert Stewart, first Duke of Albany, Guardian of Scotland on behalf of the captive James I. The principal feature is the four-storey keep-gatehouse which rises 95 ft high. It is flanked by a five-storey round tower, and the small ruined structure corbelled out from it on the left (first floor) is in fact a privy and not a doorway.

DOUNE CASTLE, THE RETAINERS' HALL 1899 44649
Situated to the right of the keep-gatehouse is the retainers' hall, a long building with a solid semi-circular bastion halfway along its length. The bastion serves several purposes. Its turreted top offered an additional defensive position from which flanking fire could be delivered along the wall to either side. Its solid bulk provided additional support for the roof.

DOUNE CASTLE 1899 44647

Robert died in 1420, and his lands and titles passed to his son Murdoch. In 1424 James returned to Scotland after spending eighteen years as the 'guest' of the English court. He was also angry; angry that Robert Stewart had done precious little to secure his freedom. With the first Duke already in his grave, revenge fell upon Murdoch and other members of the Stewart family. Arrested, tried for treason and condemned, Murdoch Stewart died by the axe on Heading Hill, Stirling. Doune was used as a royal residence until 1528 when it was returned to a descendant of Albany.

DOUNE CASTLE, THE LORD'S HALL 1899 44648
Here we see the western end of the lord's hall following its restoration. The work included relaying the floor with red, black and buff tiles based on the recovered fragments of the originals, and the fitting of oak wall panelling, the screen and the music gallery. It was from here that the portcullis was operated. When Doune was first built there were no interconnecting doorways between the keep-gatehouse and the retainers' hall.

DRUMMOND CASTLE 1899 44359
Situated 3.5 miles south-south-west of Crieff, Drummond Castle was originally built by John, first Lord Drummond in 1491. It has endured its share of troubles. It was besieged and bombarded by Cromwell; destroyed in 1689 and subsequently rebuilt; garrisoned by Hanoverian troops in 1715; and partially dismantled in 1745 by the Jacobite Duchess of Perth to deny it to the English and their allies.

DRUMMOND CASTLE, THE GARDENS 1904 52938

The gardens were originally laid out in the 17th century by John, second Earl of Perth and relaid in the early decades of the 19th century. The layout shown here dates from 1840. Drummond Castle Gardens is noted for its many rare shrubs and trees, but it also has another unusual feature. The obelisk-type structure seen here in the centre of the garden pathway is in fact a multiple sundial, which in 1904 gave the time for what were then the major cities of Europe.

DUART CASTLE
Mull 1903 M114001

Situated on a rocky site at the entrance to the Sound of
Mull, the Maclean fortress of Duart dates from the 13th
century with 16th- and 17th-century additions. The
Macleans sided with Graham of Claverhouse when he raised
the standard of James VII, and the clan held out against the
forces of William and Mary until 1691. In 1715 they fought
for the Stewart cause at Killicrankie and Sherrifmuir; their
loyalty to the King Over The Water was punished by the
Campbells. In 1745 they fought for Prince Charles Edward,
though it has been said that the core of this army was made
up of clans hoping more to settle old scores with Argyll and
the Campbells than worry too much about restoring the
house of Stewart. Following the '45, Duart was garrisoned
by government troops, but was abandoned by the end of
the 18th century and allowed to fall into ruin. It was
eventually bought back by the Macleans
and has been restored.

DUMBARTON CASTLE 1897 39809

Dumbarton Castle straddles the 240 ft high basalt rock that dominates the burgh. Protected on three sides by water, the rock was the ideal location for a fortification; for around six hundred years it was the capital of the Kingdom of Strathclyde. The oldest remains today is a 12th-century gateway; most of the buildings date from the 17th and 18th centuries.

DUNNOTTAR CASTLE
c1900 D80401

It was Sir William Keith, Marischal of Scotland, who built a
tower house at Dunnottar in the late 14th century, and is
said to have been excommunicated for his troubles by the
Bishop of St Andrews for building on sacred ground - the
site had been occupied by the parish church of Dunthoyr
since the 1270s. A Bull from Pope Benedict XIII removed
the excommunication when Sir William built another
church. The site, an isolated 150 ft high rock, is ideal for a
fortress. The tower house is of the L-plan type and dates
from the same period as that at Craigmillar Castle. The
tower is separated from the rest of the fortress by a deep
ditch, wall and gatehouse. Dunnottar was equipped for
artillery, though the military efficiency of the frontal battery
is open to question, as the guns could not be brought to
bear on the entrance. The corner tower, however, is
equipped with wide-mouthed ports allowing the defenders
to cover any attempt to climb the slopes. Following Charles
II's defeat at Worcester, Dunnottar was the only fortress
over which the royal standard of the house of Stewart
remained flying. In May 1652 Dunnottar was besieged by
General Lambert for eight months in an attempt to seize
the Royal Regalia of Scotland and the King's private papers.
The Regalia were smuggled out under the skirts of the
minister of Kinneff's wife, and the papers by Anne Lindsey.

DUNOLLIE CASTLE, OBAN 1903 50779
Situated on the northern outskirts of Oban, Dunollie was a MacDougal fortress in the 11th century. The castle's defences are enhanced by sea on three sides. It was besieged in 1647 and again in 1715; on the latter occasion it was held by the chieftain's wife against the Argyll Militia.

DUNOON CASTLE 1897 39831
This was once the seat of the Fitzalans, hereditary High Stewards of Scotland. Walter Fitzalan married Bruce's daughter Marjory, and it was their son who was crowned Robert II, thus starting the Stewart dynasty. Upon Robert's accession the Campbells were appointed hereditary keepers of Dunoon. The knight's fee is 'one red rose when asked for'. All that survives of this fortress is the rock upon which it stood and a few traces of masonry.

DUNSTAFFNAGE CASTLE 1903 50886
Situated on a rocky promontory four miles north of Oban where the waters of Loch Etive and the Firth of Lorne meet, Dunstaffnage was built on the orders of Alexander II. The site itself is ancient: it was once the capital and principal fortress of the Dalriadic kings, and the place where the Stone of Destiny was said to have been housed before its removal to Scone.

DUNSTAFFNAGE CASTLE, 1901 47518

DUNSTAFFNAGE CASTLE
1901
Dunstaffnage belongs to the period when a determined effort was being made to extend royal power. The original fortress was to be used as a forward base for an assault against the Norse-controlled Hebrides. It was equipped with a high curtain wall 10 ft thick and round towers.

◆

EDINBURGH CASTLE
from Prince's Garden 1897
This view shows some of the 18th-century buildings and defences. Butt's Battery (1708-13) is just out of the picture on the lower right. The large building in the centre is one of the twin ordnance stores (1753-54) built either side of the magazine. To the left of that is the Mills Mount Cart Shed (1746) which was later used as a barracks.

EDINBURGH CASTLE, FROM PRINCE'S GARDEN 1897 39119

EDINBURGH, THE TOMB OF THE MARQUESS OF MONTROSE 1897 39130

James Graham, fifth Marquess of Montrose was one the greatest tacticians of the Civil War. Fighting for Charles I, Montrose won victory after victory, often against overwhelming odds. His luck finally ran out at Philliphaugh in September 1645. Returning from the Continent to raise an army in support of Charles II, he was betrayed to the Covenanters and hung, drawn and quartered at Edinburgh on 21st May 1650.

EDINBURGH CASTLE 1897 39121A
The Esplanade-cum-parade ground was laid out in its present form in the 1820s. Of the castle buildings, on the left is the palace (reconstructed 1617), the Half-Moon Battery and Forewall Battery. The small tower on the right with the angled roof is the Portcullis Gate, the upper part of which was added 1886-87.

EDINBURGH CASTLE FROM THE GRASSMARKET 1897 39121
Here we get an idea of the imposing bulk of the great
Half-Moon Battery, the parapet of which was added in
the 1690s. Behind the battery is the palace and the Great
Hall; the latter was completed in the early 1500s. On this
side of the castle are most of the buildings constructed
before 1625 which have survived above ground level
in a recognisable form.

EDINBURGH CASTLE, MONS MEG c1950 E24001

James III inherited his father's passion for heavy ordnance and commissioned the construction of Mons Meg, a brute of a weapon for its time that made a great hole in James's defence budget as well as anything it was fired at. Deploying Meg was a logistical nightmare: when James IV ordered it dragged to the siege of Norham Castle in 1497, it took over 220 men and ninety horses to get it there.

EDINBURGH, FROM THE CASTLE 1897 39101

The waters of Nor' Loch once flowed over the area now occupied by Princes Gardens, the railway, and Princes Street, and together with an area of marshland formed a part of the castle and the old city's defences. The picture gives us an indication of the size of the loch.

EDINBURGH, FROM THE CASTLE c1955 E24002

When the Duke of Gordon held the castle for James VII during the 'Long Siege' of 1689, there would have been few, if any, buildings between the fortress and the port of Leith. Gordon surrendered the castle on 13 June 1689 owing to sickness and acute shortages of food and water. During 1988-91, excavations unearthed the remains of some of the garrison from this siege. None of the skeletons showed signs of wounds, but all appeared to have died from disease.

EDINBURGH, HERIOT'S HOSPITAL 1897 39135

Begun by William Wallace, principal mason to the Crown in 1627, and completed by William Aitoun in 1650, Heriot's Hospital is the direct ancestor of Drumlanrig Castle. Designed on the courtyard plan with a turreted tower house at each corner, this building echoes Wallace's work at Pinkie (1613), the King's Lodging, Edinburgh Castle (1615), and the north range at Linlithgow (1620).

HERMITAGE CASTLE 1890 23097

Lord de Soulis, who held Hermitage, met with a bizarre end. Said to be a devotee of the black arts, he was abducted by his God-fearing tenants, rolled in a sheet of lead and taken to Ninestane Rig, a stone circle beyond Whitterhope Burn. There he was put upon a fire and melted alive.

INVERLOCHY CASTLE
c1890 I30001

The 13th-century fortress at Inverlochy is a quadrangular enceinte with a round tower at each of the angles; the largest of these is known as Comyn's Tower, and forms the donjon. It was here on 2 February 1645, after a forced march covering 30 miles in 36 hours over difficult terrain in some of the worst weather in living memory, that the great Marquess of Montrose, with fewer than 2000 men, defeated a much larger force of Covenanters, Campbells and Lowlanders. Despite getting off several volleys, the Lowlanders simply disintegrated under the impact of an attack by Montrose's Irish troops led by Alistair MacColla. The Campbells fought well, but Montrose's Highlanders fought the better: this was a time for clans to settle accounts with the Campbells. The Covenanter field commander Sir Duncan Campbell of Auchinbreck was among the dead, though his superior, the Duke of Argyll, had seen fit to remain upon his galley in the loch during the whole proceedings. The banks of Loch Linnhe and Loch Eil were strewn with Covenanter dead as the Highlanders hunted down Campbell fugitives from the battle. Auchinbreck's musketeers, who had been positioned on the ramparts of the castle, were happy enough to surrender on terms. Argyll and Auchinbreck alike must have sensed that the day would be hard the moment they saw the royal standard and heard Montrose's pipers playing that quaint Cameron ditty 'Sons of dogs, come and we will give you flesh'. It is said that Inverlochy destroyed the clan power of Argyll for a generation.

INVERNESS FROM THE CASTLE c1890 I255003
There has been a fortification of one sort or another at
Inverness since the time of King Brude in the 6th century.
The first stone castle was built by David I; it was extensively
modified around 1411 following the sack of the town by the
Lord of the Isles the previous year. In 1562 Mary, Queen of
Scots was denied entry into the castle, which was then
besieged and taken by clans loyal to her. For his treason the
Governor was executed. The present castle is 19th-century.
Construction began in 1834 and was completed by 1846.

KILCHURN CASTLE, LOCH AWE c1955 I15001

KILCHURN CASTLE
Loch Awe c1955

Situated at the north east of Loch Awe, Kilchurn is a 15th-century tower built by Sir Colin Campbell of Glenorchy. Additional buildings were added on the south and north sides during the 16th and late 17th centuries respectively; these in turn created an irregular courtyard to what had been a free-standing tower. The castle was damaged during the same storm in 1879 that destroyed the Tay Bridge.

◆

LINLITHGOW PALACE
1897

David I built a manor at Linlithgow, and next to it a church dedicated to St Michael. In 1301 Edward Longshanks set about rebuilding and heavily fortifying the palace. It remained in English hands until the autumn of 1313, when it fell by deception.

LINLITHGOW PALACE, 1897 39154

LINLITHGOW PALACE 1897 39155
Situated half-way between Edinburgh and Stirling, Linlithgow became a favourite royal residence, though during the wars with the English it was often under siege or counter-siege. Mary, Queen of Scots was born here in 1542, and Prince Charles Edward Stuart stayed here in 1745. The palace was accidentally burnt down by General Hawley's troops in 1746.

LINLITHGOW PALACE, FROM THE BOAT STATION 1897 39153
Linlithgow reached its final form during the reign of
James V, though the north wing was reconstructed in the
neo-classical style between 1618-1633. The last Scottish
national parliament was held here in 1646, and Oliver
Cromwell lived at Linlithgow for several months following
the Battle of Dunbar. Also in this picture is St Michael's
Church, which was rebuilt in the 15th century.

LINLITHGOW PALACE
Queen Margaret's Bower 1897 39156

The royal apartments were situated on the west side of the quadrangle. It was here that Queen Margaret kept vigil whilst James IV fought at Flodden. James was between a rock and a hard place. He was bound to France by the 'auld alliance', and also to England by an accord signed in 1502. Despite attempts to remain out of the coming war between England and France, he was eventually drawn into it. In August 1513 a Scottish force under Lord Home raided Northumberland, but was defeated when ambushed by Sir William Bulmer of Brancepeth. Flodden would be an even worse disaster for Scottish arms. There, losses ran into thousands, and included 300 knights, nineteen barons, ten earls, a bishop and an archbishop. Worse still, a half-naked corpse was later identified as being that of James IV. The body was disembowelled, embalmed and sent to London. Catherine of Aragon was all for sending the corpse to Henry VIII who was campaigning in France, but instead it was sent to the Monastery of Sheen where it eventually finished up being dumped in a lumber room. The remains were rediscovered by workmen some time after the Dissolution; it is said that they cut off the head and used it as a football. Before it was finally laid to rest in an unmarked grave, the King's disembodied head was kept as a curio by Lancelot Young, master glazier to Elizabeth I.

LOCH LEVEN CASTLE C1890 L2355001

Though there was a castle here that withstood a siege in 1335, the five-storey tower-house dates from the late 14th to early 15th century. The entrance to the tower is on the second floor and reached only by a ladder. Loch Leven has a small irregular courtyard, known as a barmkin, which is enclosed by a curtain wall. Mary, Queen of Scots was imprisoned here by the lords of the Congregation in 1567 and compelled to abdicate in favour of her son James VI. The following year she escaped and joined her army, which was commanded by the fifth Earl of Argyll.

LOCHRANZA CASTLE, ARRAN c1890 A93001
Lochranza dates from the late 13th century to mid
14th century with 16th-century additions, and features
one of the earliest examples of an added jamb or wing
which was built on to increase the castle's defence
capability. The square tower projects to cover the
entrance, and is equipped with long arrow slits of an
early design. The original entrance was of the heavily
ribbed barrel-vaulted type.

ROSLIN CASTLE 1897 39165

Founded by Sir William Sinclair, Roslin dates from the early 14th century. Sir William's grandson built a keep which was enlarged by the third Earl of Orkney in the 1440s. During the English invasion of 1544 the castle was effectively destroyed, but was rebuilt in 1580. Further additions were made during the 17th century.

ROSLIN CASTLE 1897 39166

Henry VIII was desperate for his son Edward to be married to the infant Mary, daughter of Mary of Guise. The match was agreed in 1543, thanks to the Protestant second Earl of Arran who seems to have bullied or bribed the Scottish parliament into accepting it. Mary of Guise was against it, as was the Catholic Church, and Arran not only changed sides but also faiths. The English invaded. Edinburgh fell, Holyrood was burnt. In 1544 the English were back, burning five towns, sacking 243 villages, and destroying Roslin Castle.

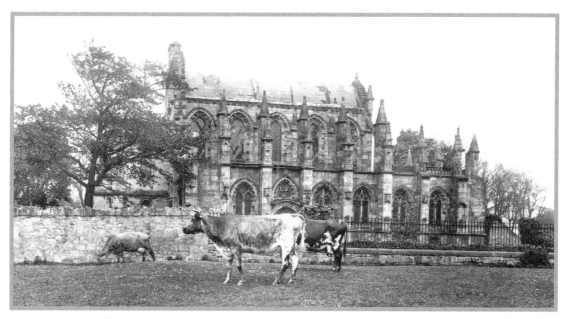

ROSLIN CHAPEL 1897 39164

Roslin Chapel was built by Sir William Sinclair, third Earl of Orkney in 1446. It is famed for a carved pillar featuring entwined ribbands. The story is that whilst the chief stonemason was away in Italy studying a similar pillar, his apprentice set to and made the one at Roslin after having a dream of how to do it. When the mason returned, he was so jealous of the lad's work that he killed him on the spot.

ROTHESAY CASTLE 1897 39845

The forework is a high tower which extends into the moat and dates from the remodelling of the castle by James IV and James V. The tower served a dual purpose; it was both a strong gatehouse and royal apartments.

ROTHESAY CASTLE 1897 39844

Described in 1549 as 'the round castle of Buitte callit Rosay of the auld', the first stone castle was a circular shell keep 142 ft in diameter with walls 30 ft high and 9 ft thick; four projecting drum towers were added in the 13th century. The design is unique. The original parapet survives, embedded in the stonework of the subsequent heightening of the curtain.

STIRLING CASTLE 1899 44696

When the forework was remodelled for James IV, it partially followed the line of earlier defences. The main gatehouse was supported by flanking half-drum towers and the curtain wall had a rectangular tower at each end, though they were of different sizes due to the geography of the site.

STIRLING CASTLE, THE GREAT HALL 1899 44697

The Napoleonic Wars led to a severe shortage of barrack accommodation in Scotland. Additional space was found by remodelling the Great Hall to create twelve barrack rooms. The work included inserting additional floors, cross walls, staircases, windows and doorways.

STIRLING CASTLE 1899 44691
To the left of the gatehouse can be seen the royal palace of James V, which abuts James IV's Prince's Tower. During the 1530s James V spent a large amount of money refurbishing Stirling as well as building a new palace. The design is thought to be French-influenced; several of the king's masons were of French origin, and two were Dutch.

STIRLING CASTLE, FROM KING'S KNOT 1899 44693
Stirling was to change hands a number of times during the Wars of Independence. In 1299 Edward I failed to relieve the garrison besieged by John Comyn, Lord of Badenoch and Bishop Lamberton of St Andrews. The Constable, John Sampson, was eventually forced to surrender.

STIRLING CASTLE
From Abbey Craig 1899 44677

It was from the southern slope of Abbey Craig that Wallace launched his attack against the Earl of Surrey's troops as they attempted to cross the narrow wooden bridge over the Forth. To save time, and money, Hugh de Cressingham, Edward I's Treasurer, had stopped Surrey exploiting a ford that would have allowed him to bring his heavy horse across the river and hit Wallace in the flank. Instead, the horse struggled to get over the bridge and deploy in line on the marshy ground on the other side. The English were cut to pieces. Surrey fled the field; the corrupt and unlikeable Cressingham knew how to die, and fought until he was cut down. It is said that his skin was flayed from his body, and that some of it was used to make a sword belt for Wallace.

STIRLING, THE BRUCE STATUE 1899 44681

Bruce's heart was carried on a crusade against the Moors of Granada by Sir James Douglas. Cut off from all support, Sir James threw Bruce's heart into the ranks of the enemy and he and his followers charged in after it. It is said that Bruce's heart was eventually returned to Scotland; it may be the mummified one interred at Melrose Abbey.

STIRLING, CAMBUSKENNETH ABBEY 1899 44699
Though not a castle, the Abbey was chosen by Bruce as a depot for his stores and reserves of ammunition prior to the Battle of Bannockburn. The Abbey was held for Bruce by Sir John Airth, but during the hours of darkness on the night of 22/23 June 1314 it was raided by the Earl of Atholl, a supporter of Edward II. Sir John's command was wiped out, giving the English king a victory of sorts.

STOBHALL CASTLE 1900 45944

Stobhall passed to Sir John Drummond in 1360. The tower, which features a corbelled stair turret, dates from 1578; this was the time when what are now termed the Z3 castles were beginning to prove popular with Scottish lords. The most numerous of the Z-plan designs, the Z3 castles had two square jambs echeloned at opposing angles from the main tower. The square shape allowed for better utilization of space.

TANTALLON CASTLE, NORTH BERWICK 1897 39187

Even in its ruined state, Tantallon still looks formidable. The great curtain wall with its central gatehouse, flanked at either end by a massive round towers, dates from the last quarter of the 14th century. The gatehouse incorporated the castellan's quarters and represents a shift away from the keep or donjon to the keep-gatehouse.

TANTALLON CASTLE 1897 39184

Tantallon was a stronghold of the Douglases, a powerful family who were wardens of the Border Marches, lords of Galloway, and by the end of the 15th century masters of much of Lothian, Stirlingshire and Clydesdale. James V resented the Douglases, and besieged Tantallon in 1528. Red Douglas held out for three months before surrendering. He was lucky to be allowed to go into exile, his estates forfeited to the Crown. Another victim of James's vendetta, Lady Glamis, was burnt at the stake for alleged witchcraft.

TANTALLON CASTLE
1897 39186

In 1388, in true Border style, the second Earl of Douglas raided the Earl of Northumberland's territory to the south as a diversionary attack durng a major incursion by the Scots. Douglas's force of around 3000 penetrated as far south as Durham, and in a clash outside Newcastle captured Northumberland's personal standard. On the evening of 19 August Northumberland, with around 7000 troops, surprised the Scots south of Otterburn. In bloody hand-to-hand fighting that went on all night the English lost over 1000 men, the Scots about 100. Douglas, however, was killed leading a charge against the Northumbrians. The Earl of Northumberland and his brother were captured.

PEEL, THE TOWN AND THE CASTLE 1893 33045

Magnus Barefoot built a timber fort on St Patrick's Isle in about 1098-1103; the bulk of the surviving fortifications date from the time of Thomas, First Earl of Derby, and were constructed in 1460-1504 as a defence against Scottish raiders. The tower in the centre of the picture overlooks the causeway linking the islet with the town, and was probably built by Sir William le Scrope in the 1390s.

PEEL CASTLE, THE ROUND TOWER 1893 33052

Built in the Irish style, the round tower dates from the 10th or 11th centuries, and would have been used by the monks as a place of refuge during raids by pirates or Vikings. Of local red sandstone, it stands 50 ft high. Originally it would have had a conical stone roof, but this was replaced by the battlemented top many centuries ago.

PEEL CASTLE

1893 33044

19th-century visitors wishing to get a good view of the town
and castle were advised to climb the tower, known as
Corrin's Folly, standing on Corrin's Hill (485ft). It was built
by a wealthy Nonconformist eccentric to the memory of his
wife and family who were buried nearby. Mr Corrin also
wanted to be buried on the hill, but he finished up in the
local churchyard. However, he had arranged with some of
his friends that if this happened they were to dig him up
and bury him near his family. This they did.

CASTLETOWN
Castle Rushen 1903

The present Castle Rushen dates from the 12th to the 14th centuries. It was here in 1265 that Magnus, the last of Man's Norse kings, died, ushering in nearly seventy years of Scottish rule until the island was taken by Edward III of England. The Doric column was erected as a memorial to Colonel Cornelious Smelt who was Lieutenant-Governor of the Island between 1805-32.

◆

CASTLETOWN
Castle Rushen 1893

In 1312 England was on the brink of civil war. Robert the Bruce seized the advantage, despatching his brother Edward and James Douglas into northern England where they sacked a number of towns. In 1313 Robert invaded Man, besieging and almost destroying Castle Rushen in the process.

CASTLETOWN, CASTLE RUSHEN 1903 50656

CASTLETOWN, CASTLE RUSHEN 1893 33021

ABBOTSFORD HOUSE 1897 39198

In 1811 Sir Walter Scott purchased the Cartley Hole estate on the banks of the Tweed and changed its name to Abbotsford. The house was designed in the baronial style by Scott himself, and built between 1817 and 1824 complete with steam central heating. It includes an armoury where Scott's collection of weapons are displayed.

ABERCAIRNY 1899 44385
Built between 1804 and 1844 by Richard Crichton and
the Dickson brothers for Charles and James Moray,
Abercairny was a break with what had become a
traditional approach to the design of country houses.
Though it features a tower, the internal arrangement
was not planned around a grand staircase or central
hall, but around corridors. Similar houses include
Southill (1796-1803) and a proposed design for
Mamhead (1822).

ABERCAIRNY 1899 44384

The house was famed for the way in which the designers successfully blended medieval and modern styles, and the prolific use of white and gold for the interiors. By late Georgian times there were three rival central heating systems available: steam, hot air, and hot water. Abercairny was fitted with a ducted hot-air system in 1829, though it is not certain if it was installed throughout or confined to just a few rooms. The house was demolished in 1960.

ARDENCAPLE CASTLE, HELENSBURGH 1901 47411

A large number of country houses, many of which were called castles by their owners, have either been demolished or are shadows of their former selves. For instance, Woolmet finished up in the middle of what became a coalfield; the land surrounding both Kincraig and Melville was given over to caravans; and the Strathleven estate became an industrial estate. Ardencaple was demolished in 1957.

BALMORAL CASTLE c1890 B268001
Queen Victoria and Prince Albert first came to the Balmoral estate in 1842 as guests of Sir Robert Gordon, and on the advice of Victoria's Scottish physician Sir James Clark; both the Queen and the Prince Consort suffered from rheumatism, and it was thought that the climate of upper Deeside might do them some good.

BALMORAL CASTLE c1890 B268002
Following Sir Robert's death in 1847, his brother the
Earl of Aberdeen suggested that Victoria and Albert
might like to take over the lease on Balmoral. There
was a problem. Though Victoria was Queen Empress
of the greatest empire in history, she had little
personal wealth. The money was found to purchase
the estate, but plans to rebuild the castle looked in
doubt. Then the Queen heard that she had been left
£500,000 for her personal use in the will of the
eccentric barrister John Camden Neild.

CULDEES CASTLE, CRIEFF 1899 44376
Many historic houses in Scotland were gutted so that their owners could avoid paying rates. Many were demolished for other reasons. Of the one hundred or so buildings in Scotland associated with the Adam brothers, fewer than half survive. Fittings from Hawkhill in Edinburgh were saved by the Scottish Georgian Society just two days before the building burnt down. Culdees Castle was demolished in 1967.

EGLINTON CASTLE, KILWINNING 1904 53151
This was built for the twelfth Earl of Eglinton by John Patterson of Edinburgh in c1798. Patterson's other work included Chillingham Castle (1803) and the rebuilding of Brancepeth Castle (1817) for William Russell of Sunderland at a cost in excess of £120,000. Eglinton was the scene of the famous tournament of 1839, when knights in armour once again showed their skill at arms. The castle was gutted in c1930.

HOLYROOD PALACE
The Front Entrance 1897 39169
In August 1543 two treaties were ratified at Holyrood for
the marriage of the infant Queen Mary to Henry VIII's son
Edward. Scotland at the time was under the governorship
of James, second Earl of Arran, a Protestant. He had used
bribery, threats and possibly blackmail to persuade the
Scottish parliament to agree to the match. However, when
all seemed to be arranged James suddenly had a change of
heart and religion, and joined Mary of Guise in opposing
the wedding. Henry VIII was not too impressed and
invaded. Holyrood and the Old Town were put to the torch.

HOLYROOD PALACE AND ARTHUR'S SEAT 1897 39168
Work on the palace began during the reign of James VI, when the north-west tower was built up against the nave of Holyrood Abbey. Building continued under James V, who added a new tower and quadrangle.

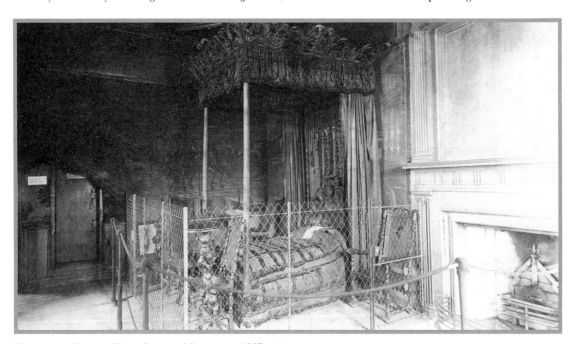

HOLYROOD PALACE, KING CHARLES' BEDROOM 1897 39172
The old four-poster with its faded canopy and drapes is kept at arms length by a wire fence and a rope. It was Charles II who ordered extensive alterations to Holyrood. Between 1670 and 1679 the quadrangle was remodelled in the French style to the designs of Sir William Bruce, the King's Surveyor in Scotland.

HOLYROOD PALACE
King Charles' Bedroom 1897
Here we see another corner of the King's bedroom. Both the bed canopy and the chair look somewhat tired, and are almost certainly dust-laden. Both have seen happier days.

◆

HOLYROOD PALACE
The Chapel Front 1897
The Abbey was founded in 1128 for the Augustinian Canons by David I, who as King was responsible for the re-introduction of monasticism into Scotland. David had no favourite order; he actively encouraged the Augustinians, Benedictines and Cistercians to open houses. Holyrood is said to have been founded by David in thanks for being spared when he was attacked by a stag whilst out hunting on a holy day.

HOLYROOD PALACE, KING CHARLES' BEDROOM *1897* 39173

HOLYROOD PALACE, THE CHAPEL FRONT 1897 39170

HOLYROOD PALACE THE CHAPEL 1897 39171
The burial place of David II, James II and James V, and described as being one of the finest examples of ecclesiastical architecture in Scotland, Holyrood Chapel was sacked during the revolution of 1688. The real damage to the Chapel occurred in 1768 when the roof fell in.

INVERARAY CASTLE c1955 I15004

The original castle at Inveraray was built about 1520.
The third Duke of Argyll decided to build a new
castle: Roger Morrison was the architect and William
Adam the clerk of works. The new site was eighty yards
or so from the old castle. Work began in 1743 and
ended in 1770. The old castle was demolished in 1773.

INVERARAY CASTLE, 1899 43204

INVERARAY CASTLE
1899

To make way for the new castle the old burgh, which was little more than a village, was demolished and a new one built. Both Morrison and Adam died long before the work was completed, their places being taken by John Adam, who supervised the works, and Robert Mylne.

MINARD CASTLE
c1955

Overlooking Minard Bay, an inlet on the north side of Loch Fyne, stands the 19th-century Minard Castle. Many other castles of the 18th and 19th centuries are no longer with us; the towered and battlemented Loudon Castle, with its sweeping raised driveway to the front entrance, built in 1811, was gutted in 1943, and Dupplin Castle was demolished in 1967.

MINARD CASTLE, c1955 F116003

MONZIE CASTLE
1899

Monzie stands to the north-west of Crieff near the village of Gilmerton. Set in parkland, the four-storey battlemented central section of the castle is supported at each corner by a three-storey round tower. There is an older building to the rear.

ROSNEATH CASTLE
1901

Built for the Duke of Argyll by J Bonomi, Rosneath was gutted in c1947 and blown up in 1961. The five-columned porte-cochere survived; it stood for a few years in the middle of what became a caravan park, until put out of its misery by the demolition men in 1964.

MONZIE CASTLE, 1899 44364

ROSNEATH CASTLE, 1901 47487

SCONE PALACE
FROM THE NORTH-WEST 1899 43914

In 1581 Scone was given to the Earl of Gowrie.
Following the forfeiture of his lands in 1600, it passed
into the ownership of Sir David Murray of Gospetrie.
He and his descendants extended the house built by
the Earl of Gowrie, but at the turn of the century the
decision was taken to build a new palace.

SCONE PALACE, FROM THE SOUTH-EAST 1899 43913

The palace was designed by William Atkinson. Work began in 1803 and finished in 1808. As with Inveraray Castle, the redevelopment meant the removal of the old village, which in this case had grown up round the Augustinian monastery destroyed in 1599. A new village of Scone was laid a mile and a half away, allowing the palace to be set in extensive parkland. All that remains of the old village are the cross and the graveyard.

SCONE PALACE, FROM THE SOUTH-WEST 1899 43916

Scone is, of course, associated with the Stone of Destiny. This measures 26 x 16 x 10 inches and is thought to have been a portable altar that once belonged to an early missionary from Iona or Ireland. The Stone, on which the kings were crowned, was brought here in 843, but was stolen by Edward I in 1296 and taken to England. It was supposed to be returned to Scotland under the terms of the Treaty of Northampton.

HOLY ISLAND C1955 H348112

A Tudor fort sitting on top of Beblowe Crag, Lindisfarne was raised for defence against the Scots. Construction began in 1542 and was completed by 1550, using stone salvaged from the Benedictine priory. The only action the castle ever saw was when it was 'captured' from its garrison of just seven men by two Jacobites, who then flew their flag for a few hours before they were eventually thrown out. The castle was demilitarised in 1819. In 1902 it was converted into a private residence for Edward Hudson by Sir Edwin Lutyens.

BAMBURGH CASTLE
c1950 B547021

A fortified site since the 6th century, the Norman castle at
Bamburgh was besieged in 1095 by William II. Unable to take the
fortress from Robert de Mowbray, third Earl of Northumberland,
William headed south, leaving the prosecution of the siege to
others. Mowbray attempted to escape but was captured. His wife
only surrendered Bamburgh after her husband had been paraded
before the walls under threat of being blinded. In July 1333
Archibald, Lord Douglas led the Scottish army in a feint towards
Bamburgh in the hopes of drawing the English away from Berwick
which they were besieging. His tactic failed, and the Scots had little
alternative but to march directly to the aid of the beleaguered
garrison. This particular siege of Berwick was ruthless. The
castellan gave his two young sons to Edward III as hostages. Edward
had inherited his grandfather's cruel streak: he executed the young
boys with neither compunction or compassion. The Scottish army
clashed with the English at Halidon Hill and was routed. Berwick
was forced to surrender. Bamburgh also holds the distinction of
being the first castle to be breached by gunfire, when forces loyal
to Edward IV deployed two large cannon. However, the garrison
was already on the point of surrendering, having eaten the last of
their horses.

ALNWICK CASTLE
The Gatehouse c1955 A223010

Alnwick has witnessed many conflicts between the Scots and the English. In 1093 Malcolm III was treacherously killed here as he leant from his saddle to accept the keys of the castle. His great-grandson William the Lion besieged Alnwick, but was captured when his horse was killed during combat with a body of English knights. William was taken before Henry II at Northampton and then shipped off to Falaise. In July 1174 William knelt in homage before Henry, swearing to hold Scotland for him as his vassal. The 11th-century castle was extended by the Percy family after they bought it in 1309. The shell keep was rebuilt by Henry de Percy, and the second Earl is thought to have built the barbican and gatehouse around 1440. Here we see the two square towers flanking the archway; these are in turn supported by a pair of octagonal towers. Between the two sets of towers there was once a moat spanned by a drawbridge.

NEWCASTLE UPON TYNE CASTLE 1901 N16022
When Robert Curthose built the New Castle on the Tyne in 1070, it marked the northern frontier of his father's kingdom. In 1092 Robert's brother William Rufus built Carlisle Castle, and it appears that a *de facto* border between England and Scotland ran between the two, probably following the line of Hadrian's wall; in those days the ruins of the wall would have been substantial. In 1812 the castle was bought by the Corporation, and it was after this date that the corner turrets and battlements were added to the keep. Also in the picture is the Black Gate, originally constructed in 1247 when the castle's defences were upgraded. The house on the top of the gate is a much later addition.

BELSAY CASTLE
c1955 B554001
Belsay, to the north west of Newcastle, is a 14th-century
Northumbrian three-storey tower with a large room on each
floor; there are other rooms off the projections. The
defensive capability of the tower parapet was enhanced by
the fitting of machicolations, an overhang that allows the
defenders to drop missiles on the heads of uninvited guests.
It is not known if Belsay was protected by a curtain wall, or if
there were any other buildings associated with the original
tower. The attached manor house was erected in 1614.

RABY CASTLE
c1955 S292006

Standing in 270 acres of parkland, Raby Castle was the seat
of the Neville family for two hundred years. It was at Raby
in 1569 that the Rising of the North was planned: the
intention was to place Mary, Queen of Scots on the throne
of England in place of Elizabeth Tudor. The plot failed, and
Raby was forfeited to the Crown. It later came into the
possession of the Vane family, though it was temporarily lost
by them to the Royalists during the English Civil War
following a surprise attack. Not to be outdone, Sir George
Vane managed to retake Raby and hold on to it, despite its
being besieged in 1648.

◆

LUMLEY CASTLE 1892 30720

Sir Robert Lumley was granted licences to crenellate
in 1389 and 1392, making Lumley, along with Raby,
County Durham's two late 14th-century castles. Each
of the four square corner towers is topped off with
octagonal machicolated turrets, from which
unpleasant things could be dropped upon the heads
of unwelcome visitors. The turreted and machicolated
gatehouse on the east side can be seen
through the trees.

DURHAM CASTLE, 1892 30759

BRANCEPETH CASTLE, 1914 67122

DURHAM CASTLE
1892

Work on the original castle began in 1072; it was the official residence of the bishops of Durham. Edward Bruce and James Douglas led a major raid into northern England in February 1312; Durham and Hartlepool were among the places sacked. Durham suffered again in 1327, and the castles of Alnwick and Norham-on-Tweed were besieged. The keep is 14th-century; it was rebuilt in 1840 to house students following the creation of Durham University in 1832. The castle was turned into a university college a few years later.

◆

BRANCEPETH CASTLE
1914

Brancepeth once belonged to the powerful Neville family, but after changing hands several times it was bought in 1796 by a wealthy Sunderland banker, William Russell. It was he and his son who spent a fortune rebuilding the castle from 1817 onwards. Most of the present buildings are 19th-century, even the Norman-style gatehouse.

SKELTON CASTLE 1891 29207

There was a castle here in the 12th century, and the family of Bruce were once lords of the manor. The present castle is a battlemented house dating from around 1800, and the seat of the Wharton family. It was the birthplace of Commander Wild, an Antarctic explorer.

BARNARD CASTLE 1898 41432

The earliest castle here is thought to have been built by Bernard de Baliol; it featured a ringwork with wooden palisading protected by an outer ditch defence. When John Baliol was crowned King of Scotland in 1292, his English estates, including Barnard Castle, were declared forfeit to the English Crown. The Bishop of Durham claimed Barnard and occupied it from 1296 to 1301; then Edward I took it back, and eventually gave it to Robert Clifford.

COCKERMOUTH CASTLE
1906 54999

Built in the mid-13th century by William de Fortibus,
Cockermouth's defences were enhanced on three sides by
its location at the junction of two rivers. A barbican
provided additional defences to the outer gatehouse on the
east side, and the inner and outer wards were divided by a
ditch, wall, and inner gatehouse equipped with a
drawbridge. The castle was besieged by the Earls of Douglas
and Fife in 1387 when they captured the town.
In September 1645 the Scots considered stationing troops
here, and the castle was in fact besieged by the Royalists
between August and September 1648.

PENRITH CASTLE
1893 32938

In 1237 the manors of Carleton, Langwathy, Scotby, Sowerby and Penrith were granted to Alexander II. Though Penrith was sacked by the Scots in 1314 and 1345, the earliest fortifications were the town walls erected in c1346-47. The Scots attacked Penrith again in 1383, but it was not until 1397 that William Strickland was granted a licence to crenellate his home that stood in the town. This was probably a pele tower, and might well have been the only stone building of any substance in Penrith at the time. A couple of years later William was granted permission to build a curtain wall and join it to his tower. The castle was enlarged by Richard, Duke of Gloucester, during his spell as Guardian of the Western March toward Scotland, but its career as a fortress was short. A 16th-century survey lists the gatehouse and gates as being in ruins and two towers and the domestic quarters as being in good repair. In 1648 Penrith was captured by the Parliamentarians, who then used it as a quarry; they partially demolished the castle and sold off the stone.

PENRITH, LOWTHER CASTLE 1894 33512
This is not so much a castle, more a country house; it was built for the first Earl of Lonsdale by Sir Robert Smirke in 1806-11. Much of the original castle burnt down in 1726, and what was left was plundered by Prince Charles Edward's men in 1745 - they also plundered the town.

KENDAL CASTLE 1896 38538
The land on which Kendal Castle stands was acquired
through marriage by Ivo de Taillebois, and it is he who
is thought to have built the original 11th-century
fortress. It was also the birthplace of Catherine Parr
(1512-1548), sixth and surviving wife of Henry VIII.
Kendal appears to have become derelict by the
beginning of the 17th century.

Index

Frith Book Co 1999 Titles

From 2000 we aim at publishing 100 new books each year. For latest catalogue please contact Frith Book Co

Barnstaple	1-85937-084-5	£12.99	Oct 99
Blackpool	1-85937-049-7	£12.99	Oct 99
Bognor Regis	1-85937-055-1	£12.99	Oct 99
Bristol	1-85937-050-0	£12.99	Oct 99
Cambridge	1-85937-092-6	£12.99	Nov 99
Cambridgeshire	1-85937-086-1	£14.99	Nov 99
Cheshire	1-85937-045-4	£14.99	Oct 99
Chester	1-85937-090-X	£12.99	Nov 99
Chesterfield	1-85937-071-3	£12.99	Oct 99
Chichester	1-85937-089-6	£12.99	Nov 99
Cornwall	1-85937-054-3	£14.99	Oct 99
Cotswolds	1-85937-099-3	£14.99	Nov 99

Northumberland & Tyne and Wear	1-85937-072-1	£14.99	Sep 99
North Yorkshire	1-85937-048-9	£14.99	Oct 99
Nottingham	1-85937-060-8	£12.99	Oct 99
Oxfordshire	1-85937-076-4	£14.99	Oct 99
Penzance	1-85937-069-1	£12.99	Oct 99
Reading	1-85937-087-X	£12.99	Nov 99
St Ives	1-85937-068-3	£12.99	Oct 99
Salisbury	1-85937-091-8	£12.99	Nov 99
Scarborough	1-85937-104-3	£12.99	Oct 99
Scottish Castles	1-85937-077-2	£14.99	Nov 99
Sevenoaks and Tonbridge	1-85937-057-8	£12.99	Oct 99
Sheffield and S Yorkshire	1-85937-070-5	£14.99	Oct 99
Shropshire	1-85937-083-7	£14.99	Nov 99
Southampton	1-85937-088-8	£12.99	Nov 99
Staffordshire	1-85937-047-0	£14.99	Nov 99
Stratford upon Avon	1-85937-098-5	£12.99	Nov 99
Suffolk	1-85937-074-8	£14.99	Nov 99
Surrey	1-85937-081-0	£14.99	Nov 99
Torbay	1-85937-063-2	£12.99	Oct 99
Wiltshire	1-85937-053-5	£14.99	Oct 99

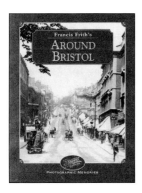
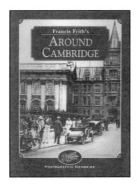

Derby	1-85937-046-2	£12.99	Oct 99
Devon	1-85937-052-7	£14.99	Oct 99
Dorset	1-85937-075-6	£14.99	Oct 99
Dorset Coast	1-85937-062-4	£14.99	Nov 99
Dublin	1-85937-058-6	£12.99	Oct 99
East Anglia	1-85937-059-4	£14.99	Oct 99
Eastbourne	1-85937-061-6	£12.99	Oct 99
English Castles	1-85937-078-0	£14.99	Oct 99
Essex	1-85937-082-9	£14.99	Nov 99
Falmouth	1-85937-066-7	£12.99	Oct 99
Hampshire	1-85937-064-0	£14.99	Nov 99
Hertfordshire	1-85937-079-9	£14.99	Nov 99
Isle of Man	1-85937-065-9	£14.99	Nov 99
Maidstone	1-85937-056-X	£12.99	Oct 99

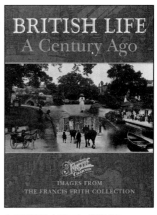

British Life A Century Ago

246 x 189mm 144pp, hardback. Black and white Lavishly illustrated with photos from the turn of the century, and with extensive commentary. It offers a unique insight into the social history and heritage of bygone Britain.

1-85937-103-5 £17.99

Available from your local bookshop or from the publisher

FRITH PRODUCTS & SERVICES

Francis Frith would doubtless be pleased to know that the pioneering publishing venture he started in 1860 still continues today. More than a hundred and thirty years later, The Francis Frith Collection continues in the same innovative tradition and is now one of the foremost publishers of vintage photographs in the world. Some of the current activities include:

Interior Decoration

Today Frith's photographs can be seen framed and as giant wall murals in thousands of pubs, restaurants, hotels, banks, retail stores and other public buildings throughout the country. In every case they enhance the unique local atmosphere of the places they depict and provide reminders of gentler days in an increasingly busy and frenetic world.

Product Promotions

Frith products have been used by many major companies to promote the sales of their own products or to reinforce their own history and heritage. Brands include Hovis bread, Courage beers, Scots Porage Oats, Colman's mustard, Cadbury's foods, Mellow Birds coffee, Dunhill pipe tobacco, Guinness, and Bulmer's Cider.

Genealogy and Family History

As the interest in family history and roots grows world-wide, more and more people are turning to Frith's photographs of Great Britain for images of the towns, villages and streets where their ancestors lived; and, of course, photographs of the churches and chapels where their ancestors were christened, married and buried are an essential part of every genealogy tree and family album.

A series of easy-to-use CD Roms is planned for publication, and an increasing number of Frith photographs will be able to be viewed on specialist genealogy sites. A growing range of Frith books will be available on CD.

The Internet

Already thousands of Frith photographs can be viewed and purchased on the internet. By the end of the year 2000 some 60,000 Frith photographs will be available on the internet. The number of sites is constantly expanding, each focussing on different products and services from the Collection.

Some of the sites are listed below.

www.townpages.co.uk
www.familystorehouse.com
www.britannia.com
www.icollector.com
www.barclaysquare.co.uk
www.cornwall-online.co.uk

For background information on the Collection look at the two following sites:

www.francisfrith.com
www.francisfrith.co.uk

Frith Products

All Frith photographs are available Framed or just as Mounted Prints, and can be ordered from the address below. From time to time other products - Address Books, Calendars, Table Mats, Postcards etc - are available.

The Frith Collectors' Guild

In response to the many customers who enjoy collecting Frith photographs we have created the Frith Collectors' Guild. Members are entitled to a range of benefits, including a regular magazine, special discounts and special limited edition products.

For further information: if you would like further information on any of the above aspects of the Frith business please contact us at the address below:

The Francis Frith Collection, Frith's Barn, Teffont, Salisbury, Wiltshire England SP3 5QP.
Tel: +44 (0) 1722 716 376 Fax: +44 (0) 1722 716 881   Email: uksales@frithbook.co.uk

To receive your FREE Mounted Print

Cut out this Voucher and return it with your remittance for £1.50 to cover postage and handling. Choose any photograph included in this book. Your SEPIA print will be A4 in size, and mounted in a cream mount with burgundy rule lines, overall size 14 x 11 inches.

Order additional Mounted Prints at HALF PRICE (only £7.49 each*)

If there are further pictures you would like to order, possibly as gifts for friends and family, acquire them at half price (no additional postage and handling required).

Have your Mounted Prints framed*

For an additional £14.95 per print you can have your chosen Mounted Print framed in an elegant polished wood and gilt moulding, overall size 16 x 13 inches (no additional postage and handling required).

---

* IMPORTANT!

These special prices are only available if ordered using the original voucher on this page (no copies permitted) and at the same time as your free Mounted Print, for delivery to the same address

---

Frith Collectors' Guild

From time to time we publish a magazine of news and stories about Frith photographs and further special offers of Frith products. If you would like 12 months FREE membership, please return this form and we will send you a New Member Pack.

Send completed forms to:
The Francis Frith Collection, Frith's Barn, Teffont, Salisbury, Wiltshire SP3 5QP

Voucher for FREE and Reduced Price Frith Prints

Picture no.	Page number	Qty	Mounted @ £7.49	Framed + £14.95	Total Cost
		1	**Free of charge***	£	£
			£	£	£
			£	£	£
			£	£	£
			£	£	£
			£	£	£

	* Post & handling	£1.50
	Total Order Cost	£

Title: SCOTTISH CASTLES
   077-2

Please do not photocopy this voucher. Only the original is valid, so please cut it out and return it to us.

I enclose a cheque / postal order for £ . . . .
made payable to 'The Francis Frith Collection'
OR please debit my Mastercard / Visa / Switch / Amex card

Number . . . .

Expires . . . . Signature . . . .

Name Mr/Mrs/Ms . . . .

Address . . . .

. . . .

. . . .

. . . .

. . . . Postcode . . . .

Daytime Tel No . . . .   Valid to 31/12/01

The Francis Frith Collectors' Guild

I would like to receive the New Members Pack offering 12 months FREE membership.
                                                                077-2

Name Mr/Mrs/Ms . . . .

Address . . . .

. . . .

. . . .

. . . . Postcode . . . .

Free Print - see overleaf